AF248680

Sportsviewers Guide
SNOOKER

Peter Bills

DAVID & CHARLES
Newton Abbot   London

Contents

History and Development 4–7
How a game with royal roots first flowered in the British Raj in India and captured the imagination of people all over the world.

Rules and Terminology 8–13
The set-up, scoring and rules of the game are backed up by a list of terms from 'baulk' to 'touching ball'.

The Stars 14–39
A dossier on 20 top stars from Joe Davis, the first household name in snooker, to his unrelated namesake, Steve Davis.

Road to the top 40–43
Practice and competition from an early age are the only answer for the young hopeful, who must master the techniques and the tension at junior and amateur level before he can consider entering the professional ranks.

Events 44–47
The Embassy world championships every spring are the pinnacle of the professional's ambitions but the growing fixture list is a sign of snooker's popularity among spectators and sponsors, even in times of recession.

Venues 48–51
The Crucible Theatre, Sheffield, has become the home of the world championship but the tournament and exhibition circuit takes the players all over Britain and to the far corners of the world.

Equipment 52–57
This section includes a run-down on the equipment from tables to tips, cues to rests.

People in the media 58–61
Ted Lowe's velvet voice has been associated with snooker on TV since the early days of BBC'S *Pot Black*.

Statistics 62–63

British Library Cataloguing in Publication Data
Bills, Peter
    Snooker. — (Sportsviewers guides)
    1. Snooker — History
    I. Title   II. Series
    794.7'35'09   GV900.S6

    ISBN 0–7153–8506–2

The Sportsviewers' Guide to Snooker was produced and designed by Siron Publishing Limited of 20 Queen Anne Street, London W1
Series editor: Nicholas Keith
Photographs by Tommy Hindley and Tony Henson of Professional Sport

Typeset by ABM Typographics Ltd, Hull and printed by
Printer Industria Grafica SA
Cuatro Caminos, Apartado 8,
Sant Vicenç dels Horts,
Barcelona, Spain DLB 17339-1983
for David & Charles (Publishers) Limited
Brunel House   Newton Abbot   Devon

Foreword

Snooker! The word alone conjures up a world of immaculately dressed men with impeccable manners, capturing a huge sporting audience of millions of TV viewers. This would have seemed impossible in 1969 when *Pot Black* first appeared on BBC2, but this only whetted the appetites of millions of people about to become addicted to the game over the next fifteen years. A world of skill, elegance and — perhaps most important in a world of diminishing values — true sportsmanship.

This book reveals how a game which started in the far-flung reaches of the British Raj progressed to become the vastly popular sport it is today.

Players' achievements are today internationally recognised; information on your favourites which has made them into household names — more familiar to the British public than newscasters and politicians — is recorded. Included is a comprehensive section on venues, equipment, rules and terminology, plus a piece on the unsung heroes like 'Whispering' Ted Lowe whose dulcet tones have guided us through some of the most exciting snooker ever seen, together with his fellow commentators.

Of all the snooker books I have read, this one encapsulates all one needs to know, making it a MUST for fan or collector.

History and development

Research into the origins of snooker reveals a strong historical link with military matters in all corners of the world. Snooker is a development from the game of billiards, although it originated comparatively recently — little more than one hundred years ago. Such are the unmistakeable links between the two games that no history of snooker would be complete without some sketch of how billiards came into being.

In keeping with the importance of military affairs and personnel in centuries past, billiards had a close liaison with war and fighting men. The Romans played a game with long sticks and rounded balls but exact connections between that and snooker/billiards are understandably hazy.

There are links between billiards and the old French game of Paille Maille which in turn has close affiliations with the game we know as croquet. There seems little doubt that billiards was played outdoors at some stage so that the development of croquet is not hard to understand. When billiards moved indoors, it began to take on undisputed characteristics of its own and developed its own particular pattern.

We believe the word 'billiards' comes originally from the French word which means a curved stick. The term cue probably derives from another French word, *queue,* which means tail. 'Billiard' is mentioned in French literature as far back as 1550 and it is believed that English kings such as Henry III enjoyed the game, probably while on their campaigns in France. Henry IV, who built some fine French castles such as the one at Pau in the south-west of France, would also have played the game abroad.

So the association between the game and the English gradually grew as warriors and kings returning from foreign fields introduced the game to a growing audience at home. The game was enjoyed by the nobility, because the size of the table required large rooms. The homes of ordinary folk are most unlikely to have had room for the game.

From the days when a mace was used to strike the balls in croquet style the cue gradually came into being. But it was not a cue as we know it today — more probably, a rough stick or length of wood with a rounded edge and without the modern leather tip covered in chalk.

The development of the tip is generally credited to a prisoner of the French Revolution, Captain Mingaud, who, by some extraordinary means, managed to get a billiard table delivered into his cell at the infamous Bastille where he was imprisoned. The captain spent his time in prison developing the game he enjoyed so much. The whole story seems somewhat bizarre for, in other parts of the city, similar connections with the French nobility were being destroyed by the revolutionaries. Anyway, Mingaud's lengthy experiments led to the cue with tip and, at a slightly later date, a leather tip with chalk used as an aid.

Billiards became popular in several countries and yielded the offshoot of snooker. We can tell with rather more certainty of snooker's birth and growth. Snooker was introduced to the world by the British during the days of the Raj in India.

British officers playing traditional billiards decided to experiment in the hope of making the game more varied. The idea was to add excitement; it is strange, in some respects, that a game played traditionally with three balls should have retained its staid format for several centuries before anyone had the bright idea of livening things up by devising one featuring more balls.

Anyone for billiards? The Duchess de Bourgogne at play in about 1700. Note the 'maces' and the hoops as in croquet.

History and development/2

English officers in an Indian Army mess — Sir Neville Chamberlain among them — are credited with the idea. The term 'snooker' was not complimentary in those days. It is believed to have been used by Sir Neville at Jubbulpore (now Jabalpur) in 1875 when one of his opponents left him an unplayable shot. He is said to have accused his opponent of being 'a regular snooker' — a derogatory term for a first-year cadet at the Woolwich Military Academy.

Chamberlain may well have suggested the name in jocular fashion but, whatever its original intent, the name and the game stuck. More balls were added by the English gentlemen at the club in the hills of India, probably in Ootacamund (known as 'Ooty') and keen billiards players travelled from England to India to learn more of Sir Neville's idea.

Billiards in its traditional form did have limitations in terms of excitement and variety. The cue was king in the hands of an expert and games often became monotonous. Snooker was more exciting mainly because there were so many more balls on the table. From the times when surfaces were rough and the sides of the table made from lumps of wood, merely as a device to keep the balls on the table, the game developed apace. Wooden tables were replaced by slate-bed models and, eventually, the cushioned sides capable of giving perfect rebounds were introduced.

From 1875, the year of its inception, snooker caught on rapidly. By 1927, Joe Davis, a player who was to become a household name in so many parts of the world, had organised the first world professional championship, which he won. Davis was in a class of his own in those days, winning that world title every year until 1940 when the event was suspended because of the Second World War. He resumed

his run of success after the war, winning the title once more in 1946 before retiring undefeated. Davis, whose brother Fred was destined to become as famous in later years, also won the world billiards title from 1928 to 1932.

Since then, snooker has spread in popularity in all countries. The war years, as has proved to be the case in so many examples of sports development, helped snooker to gain in popularity among the working classes. Tables were set up in army messes and public houses and the game was enjoyed by servicemen on leave or during off-duty periods in their barracks.

After the war, the game continued to prosper, although it was not until television took an interest that players were able to make such a handsome living from the professional game. By that time, players like Fred Davis, acknowledged as one of the

Calm before the storm: no sign of any 'Hurricanes' in this after-dinner game at the turn of this century.

early masters, had had his day to a large extent, although even in the 1980s the splendid old master still competes in the big televised events at the age of seventy. So from a noble heritage in English and French courts, snooker has travelled the world, into the homes of many, and is now in reach of all sections of society.

The modern snooker explosion has developed since the arrival of colour television. Joe Davis was involved in a number of challenge matches in black and white but television companies lost interest and snooker disappeared from the small screen for a while in the mid-1960s. *Pot Black* started in 1969 with a TV audience of 1m–2m and the 1983 final between Steve Davis and Ray Reardon attracted 9.2m viewers.

The early years of colour presentation were dogged by problems with the brightness of the lights. Ray Reardon was involved in a number of argu-ments over the lights and in the 1970s Nick Hunter, a BBC producer, saw to it that lights were devised which suited the players as well as the TV cameras. Hunter was also the man responsible for developing the extended coverage of snooker, with blanket screening being substituted gradually for excerpts and highlights.

The 1983 world championships had 80 hours of TV exposure. Although many people believe that this amounts to 'overkill' and could be bad for the game, there is no arguing with the consistently high viewing figures. The last week of the tournament had an average audience of 6m and eight of the top ten BBC2 programmes were snooker transmissions. This represents a fall from the audience of over 15m who watched one session of the 1981 world final, but it is a respectable figure in days of declining viewing figures for TV sport.

Rules/1

As we have seen snooker employs several more balls than its parent sport, billiards. Snooker is played on a pocket billiard table with the white cue-ball, fifteen red balls (scoring value 1) and six other coloured balls ('colours') — from the lowest value upwards they are yellow (2), green (3), brown (4), blue (5), pink (6) and black (7).

The balls are arranged at set positions on the table; the cluster of red balls in the shape of a triangle at one end of the table, opposite the white cue-ball which is always the first ball to be struck. Three balls are at the far end of the table away from the original position of the reds — the brown, flanked on either side by the yellow and green. The blue ball is stationed in the middle of the table; the pink sits in front of the red balls at the top of the triangle and the black is situated just behind the pack of reds.

As long as a red ball remains on the table, the white ball (the cue-ball) must strike that red, although not necessarily with the intent of potting the ball in one of the pockets. But if a red is potted the player must next hit or pot a colour; then another red and so on until the table is cleared.

The term 'to snooker' means positioning the cue-ball behind another ball, thus blocking a clear path to the target ball. A player can force his opponent (or sometimes accidentally himself) to find another less direct path to the target ball — with a swerve shot or by playing off a cushion. This is known as a snooker or being snookered and it is a defensive ploy.

To build up a score, a player must attempt to pocket any of the red balls in any of the six pockets on the table. Having sunk a red, the player is then free to select any coloured ball he requires to add to his score. High-scoring balls, especially the black, are usually selected but by no means in every instance. A player may decide to sink a relatively low-value colour if that also makes it easier to position the cue-ball correctly for the next red.

Having sunk a colour that ball must then be put back on the table in its originally designated position. However, if the normal spot is blocked by another, the coloured ball must be put on the spot of the next highest value and left there until such time as it is sunk, thereby returning it to its original position — assuming that spot has since been vacated.

In playing any coloured ball, it is normal for the player to say which ball he is attempting. Professionals are not usually required to go through this procedure but in cases where the target ball is close to another colour, or when the path to the target ball is blocked or restricted, the referee will expect the player to name his objective.

If a player nominates a colour and fails to strike it with the cue ball he loses the value of that ball. If, in the opinion of the referee, he has deliberately missed it as a defensive ploy, the opponent has three options:
1. He can ask the referee to place the cue ball where it was originally and make the player take his shot again.
2. He can force the opponent to play again from where the cue ball now rests.
3. He can play a shot himself.

Alex Higgins was given these options in a controversial 1983 world championship match against Willie Thorne but admitted later that he did not know the rules had been changed.

Red balls which are pocketed are not replaced upon the table but count as a value of one. All coloured balls pocketed must be brought back onto the table until such time as there are no more red balls left. The only exception to this rule is when the last red ball has been potted and the player, in

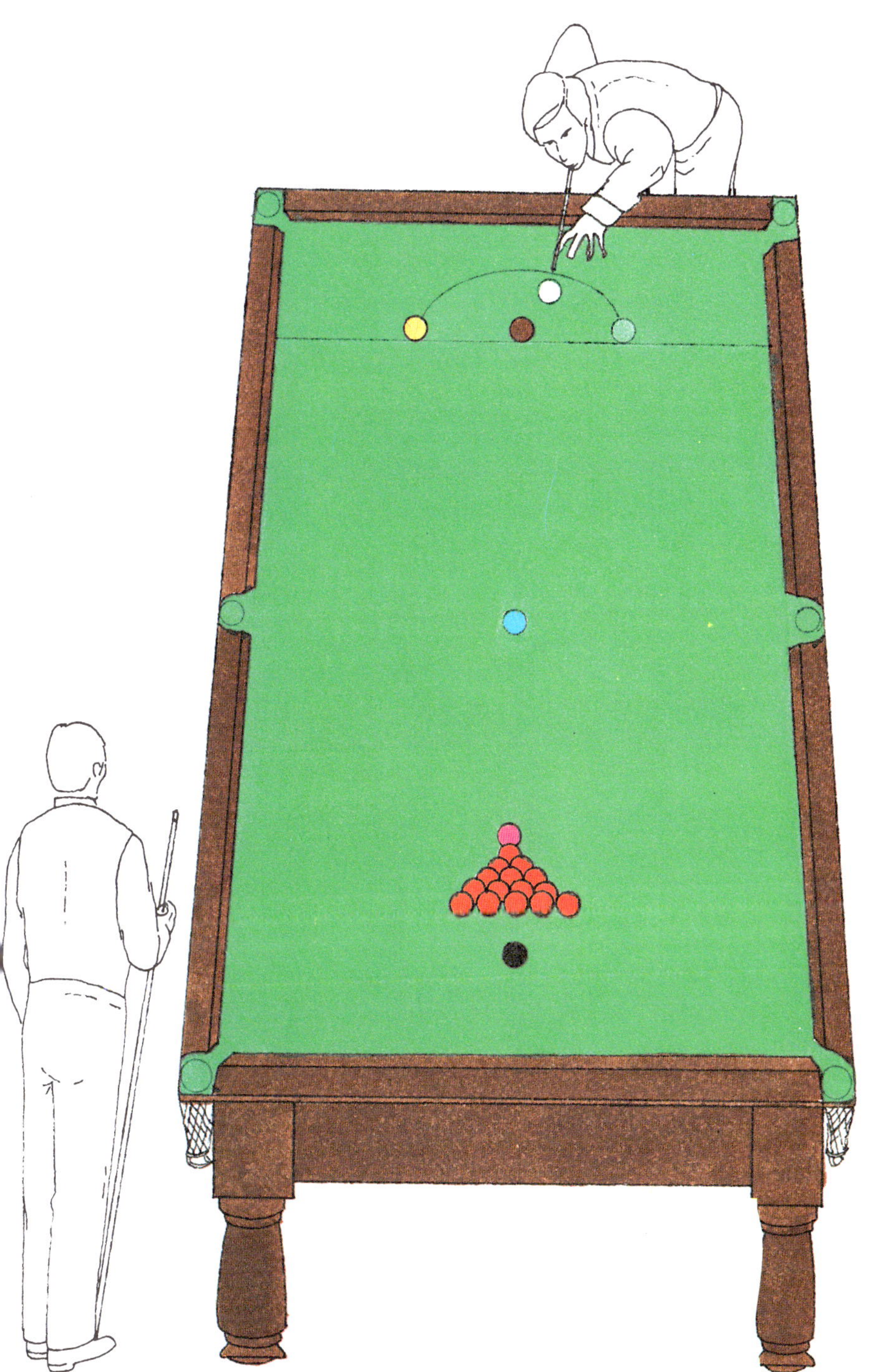

continuing his break, has followed up by sinking a coloured ball. In that case, no further reds remain on the table, but the coloured ball must still be brought back onto the table and put on its spot (or the highest value position available) for the conclusion to a frame.

To end the game, the players must pot all the coloured balls, in strict sequence in ascending order according to their values. The game is still alive, technically at least, until only the black ball remains with the white cue-ball on the table. Of course some frames are closely fought and a player may need to sink the black to win. This is known as 'a black ball game'.

If a player fails to pot a ball during a game, his break is over and his opponent comes to the table to attempt a break. If any red balls remain on the table, the player must attempt to pocket one of those before selecting a coloured ball.

The greatest difference between snooker and billiards is that the latter involves only three balls. In billiards points are won either by potting balls or playing cannons and the scoring system is radically different to snooker.

In a snooker black ball game, the first player to sink the black or incur a penalty is the winner. Any penalty on black by the player who is cueing automatically loses the game. Similarly, the first player to pot the black ball is the winner of the game, unless that black levels the scores. If so, the black is put back onto the table.

Even if red balls are pocketed illegally — ie by cannoning off a coloured ball and rolling into a pocket — they are not brought back onto the table. But the player who cued the ball in such circumstances is penalised and loses his turn at the table. Coloured balls illegally potted or sunk by mistake must always be returned to the table.

The expression 'touching ball' means that the cue ball has come to rest against another ball on the table and, regardless of the intended direction of the player's next shot, it must be directed away from the ball against which it is in contact. The other ball must not be moved; if it is, that is deemed to be 'a push shot' and is penalised.

If a player is snookered and un-intentionally hits another ball in attempting to strike his target ball, he is penalised and this is added to his opponent's score. In normal circum-stances, that would allow his opponent to come to the table but, if the cue ball is in a difficult position, the opponent may ask the player to continue at the table and solve the problem himself — this is known as 'putting your oppo-nent in again'.

In other circumstances, if an opponent is snookered by his rival's penalty stroke, he may select any ball he requires and it counts as a red —

1 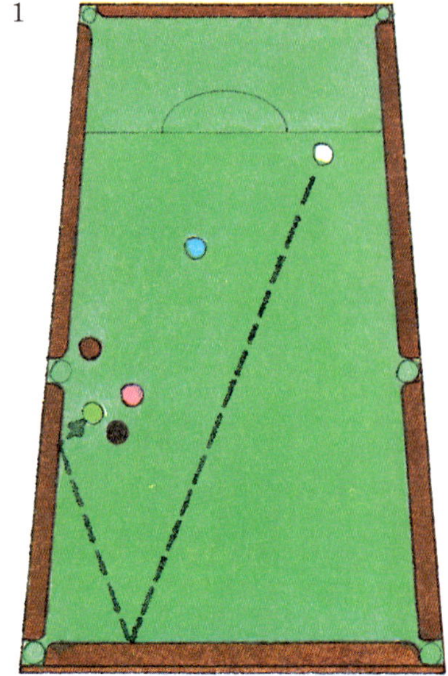

therefore scoring one. The exception to this rule is when all the reds have been pocketed and in that event the ball nominated is regarded as the target ball from which a player has been illegally snookered.

The minimum penalty score is four points. Penalties can be given for a variety of mistakes: including potting the white cue ball; sinking a ball not designated before the shot was made; missing all the balls; striking two balls simultaneously; potting two balls at once; hitting a ball clean off the table; moving another ball with part of the body in making the shot: moving a ball when the cue ball is touching it (touching ball); hitting any ball before the cue ball is struck; playing with both feet off the ground; striking a moving ball or before a potted ball has been replaced on the table; striking a ball which has been put in its wrong position; playing out of turn; making a push shot or striking the ball with anything other than the cue.

For the record the amateur snooker governing body is:-

Billiards and Snooker Control
Council,
32 John William Street,
Huddersfield,
Yorkshire.
Tel. 0484–35416.

The professional governing body is:-

World Professional Billiards &
Snooker Association,
77 Charlmont Road,
West Bromwich,
West Midlands.
Tel. 021–588–4540.

Scoring is normally done on a board which has digits of single figures, tens and hundreds. The maximum possible break is 147 — 15 reds, 15 blacks following each red plus every other colour.

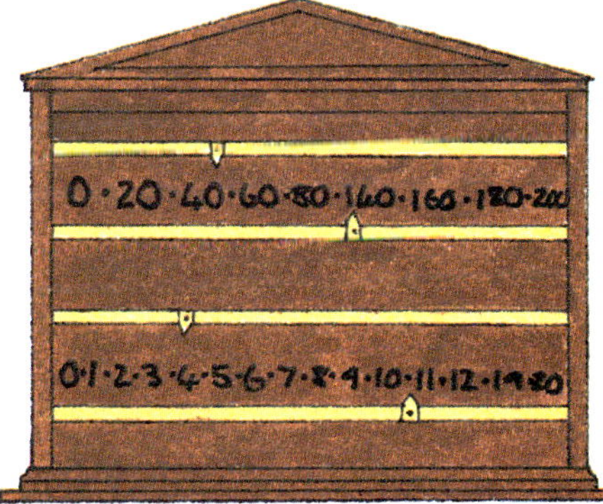

1 Snookered: the player has no clear path to the target ball and must attempt to make contact by using the cushions.

2 Jump shot: once again the player is snookered. It would be possible for a good player to make the cue ball jump over the obstructing ball to reach the target. Unfortunately this ploy is illegal.

Glossary

Baulk colours   green, brown, yellow.
Baulk cushion   top end of table
where white (cue) ball begins game.
Black ball game   when a player has
to sink the black to win the game.
Break   a sequence of shots
amounting to a score.

Cannon   hitting of two balls
successively by player's ball.
Clearance   potting all balls
remaining on table in one break.

Colour   any of the coloured balls
except red.
Cue ball   the white ball, always
struck first.
Cushion   rim around edge of table
2in wide.
In-off   when the cue-ball is potted
after sinking another ball.
Double   striking the cushion
opposite the pocket a player is aiming
for to double back.
Fluke   an unintended shot.
Frame   one game.
Half-butt   a long, extended rest.
Jumpshot   a foul by which the cue
ball is made to jump over any ball
whether by accident or design.

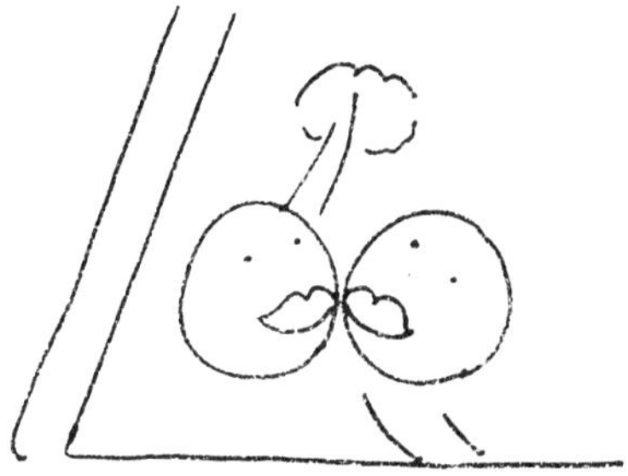

Kiss   slight deflection/touch.
Loose/open reds   broken pack of
red balls.
Miscue   mis-hit white ball.

Nap   pile of the cloth of the table, to
be brushed from baulk to spot end.
On   the ball that is to be struck next
or a ball which can be potted.
Pocket, to/pot, to   to sink a ball in
one of the six pockets.
Push shot   when the cue ball is
pushed against another rather than
hit (foul).

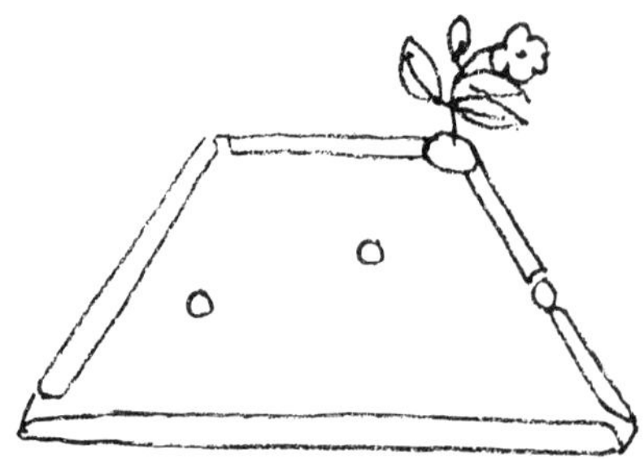

Plant   hitting the cue ball at one ball
with the intention of making it cannon
into and pot another close by.

Putting one's opponent in again
asking one's opponent to solve the
problem he has left on the table after
he has been penalised for a foul shot
after a snooker.

Side   hitting a ball with bias on one
particular side to get a spin off in the
required direction.
Snooker, to/a snooker   a player is
snookered when a ball he must not
play obstructs a straight line between
the cue ball and the target ball.

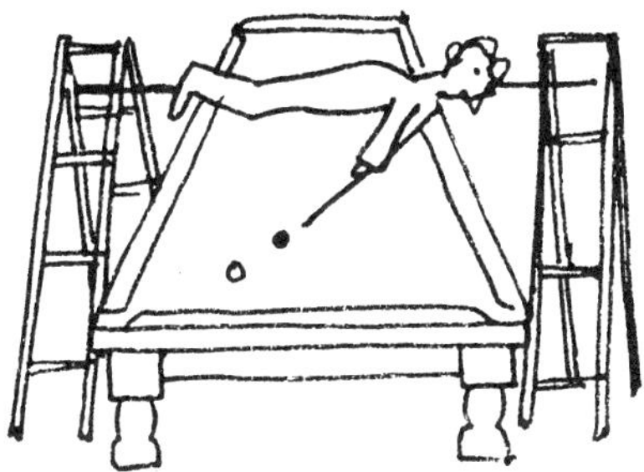

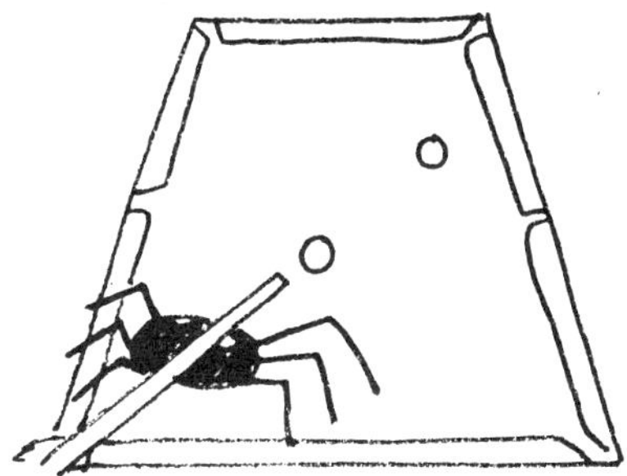

Rest   device to support cue for
certain shots.
Re-spotting   the placing on its spot
of any coloured ball that has been
pocketed while a red ball is left on the
table. Red balls are not re-spotted.
Safety shot   not attempting to sink a
ball but merely make it safe and leave
nothing 'on'.

Spider   high rest used for positions
where ordinary rest is not tall enough.
Spot   place on table belonging to a
colour.
Spot occupied   when a ball cannot
be placed in its normal position
without touching or disturbing
another ball.

Stun   use of reverse spin by striking
ball below centre.
Swerve   using considerable amount
of spin forcing ball to shape into an arc
around another.
Thin cut   the finest contact to
achieve a deflection.
Touching ball   when the cue ball
comes to rest against another ball on
the table and must be directed away
from the ball with which it is in
contact.

Screw   the spin placed on the cue
ball to gain perfect position for the
next shot.

The Stars/1

Joe Davis

The greatest ever professional, in the eyes of many, he combined a successful career as a player and as an organiser who streamlined and created the modern framework. Elder brother of Fred, Joe won the first world professional championship in 1927. He was twelve years older than Fred and set his younger brother a daunting record to follow. On 22 January 1955 Joe made the maximum 147 break in an exhibition match at the Leicester Square Hall which was recognised as a world record.

Joe won the world professional billiards championship four times, between 1928 and 1932 and held the world professional snooker title from 1927, its inaugural year, to 1946 when he relinquished the crown. He gave up championship play in 1947 at the age of forty-six when a weak right eye forced his retirement. He came from Derbyshire and began playing billiards at the age of ten. He was awarded the OBE for services to snooker. Joe Davis died on 10 July 1978 at the age of seventy-seven.

Fred Davis

Fred Davis is still a regular competitor on the world circuit after a long and fruitful career in billiards and snooker. He was born in Chesterfield, Derbyshire, in 1913 and became boys billiards champion when he was fifteen.

His natural progression to snooker followed and he lost to his elder brother Joe in the world professional final of 1940, by a single frame. But he went on to win the world title ten times. He also won the United Kingdom professional billiards title in 1951.

During his career, he had to struggle against short-sightedness for several years until being fitted with a special kind of spectacles. Not only did he become a great champion against the prediction of his elder brother — but he was also a splendid ambassador for the game. His friendliness, courtesy and impeccable manners in both victory and defeat won him admirers all over the world. He is known to this day as a great man and a great snooker player.

He was runner-up to John Spencer in the 1971 BBC *Pot Black* tournament. In 1980, he won the world professional billiards championship. He lost this title in 1982 and was beaten in the 1983 final by Rex Williams at Peterborough. He and his late brother are the only players to have won both the world billiards and world snooker tournaments. But in 1979, he lost his twenty-eight year hold on the UK professional billiards championship. He was awarded the OBE in 1977 for services to snooker.

The Stars/2

Eddie Charlton

The veteran Australian has been an almost permanent fixture on the UK snooker scene for many years. Born in a small New South Wales town in October 1929, he began by playing billiards and mastered that game before progressing to snooker.

He started playing the game at the age of nine but his work in the coal-mining town where he had grown up restricted his development into a world class player. Like many other Australians, he played a variety of sports and spent twenty-two years in the coal-mining industry.

He was a member of the Sydney Belmont surf boat crew which won the Australian title in 1950 and also played squash, golf, cricket, boxing and athletics. In snooker, he has won a host of titles in his native Australia and around the world. But he has never won the world championship although he was beaten finalist in 1968, 1973 and 1975 and has several times reached the semi-finals. He won the *Pot Black* tournament in 1972, 1973 and 1980. His home is now in Sydney; he manages a billiards company and also organises tournaments.

Ray Reardon

Ray started winning tournaments when he was only seventeen and over thirty years later he is still a successful tournament winner, as proved by his triumphs in 1983 — the Welsh professional championships, the Yamaha Organs international masters and also the professional players tournament.

He was born in 1932 in Tredegar, South Wales, and has been world champion six times, the first time in 1970. He learned the game in the valleys of South Wales, mainly from his father and uncles who all played.

He was Welsh amateur champion in 1950 and held that title for six years. He went on to win the English amateur championship in 1964. He took the first *Pot Black* title in 1969; he has won the event once subsequently and was runner-up to Steve Davis in April 1983 as well as finishing second on three other occasions. He was a member of the Welsh team which won the State Express world challenge cup in 1980. He lost the final of the 1982 world championships to Alex Higgins, a defeat which cost him the chance of his seventh world title.

Reardon has won most of the leading tournaments the game has to offer — and he has done it by retaining his friendly, sometimes jocular and lighthearted approach to tournament play. Little disturbs Reardon's calm, controlled, leisurely pace of playing; he is the complete opposite of young players like Jimmy White, whom he beat in the final of the 1983 Yamaha Organs masters.

He epitomises the phrase 'the supreme professional' with his careful potting, dedication and consistency. Few men have possessed Reardon's touch, his consistency at the highest level over the years and his modesty, which has endeared him to millions perhaps more than any other factor.

Steve Davis

A Londoner, he is not related to Joe and Fred Davis. He came from virtually nowhere to win the 1981 world championship with a remarkable display of consistent potting and brilliant positional play. In fact Davis had won tournaments in the professional ranks before that — the 1980 Coral UK professional championship and the 1981 Yamaha Organs title. But his world championship win announced him to the world as a young player with audacious skills.

He was born in Plumstead, South London, in 1957 and gradually worked his way towards the top through amateur championships. He turned professional in 1978, having won the all England junior billiards title in 1976.

Davis caused a sensation in 1980 by beating the world champion, Terry Griffiths in the second round. He won further awards in 1981, the year of his world title success, including the Jameson international and the John Courage English professional. He was BBC television's *Pot Black* champion in 1982 and retained the title in a memorable 1983 final against Ray Reardon.

If his arrival on the world stage was startling, his demise, the following year, was equally remarkable. He lost in the first round to Tony Knowles, the Bolton professional, and saw Alex Higgins go on to take his world crown.

That defeat by Knowles precipitated a setback for Davis, who lost the aura of invincibility which he had built up with his string of successes in 1981. But he returned to better form in the latter part of 1982 and 1983 although the swelling ranks of professional stars meant Davis's 1981 domination of the game was by no means as certain in the years to come.

First, Davis achieved a maximum 147 break in the 1982 Lada classic at Oldham. This was the first time the feat had been achieved in a televised tournament, but Davis lost to Griffiths in the final — the Welshman's first victory over the 'Plumstead Potter' in a big event.

A key reason for the Davis decline after his world title success was that he was so heavily committed to exhibitions and personal appearances. His manager, Barry Hearn, had fixed contracts with Leisure Industries (£100,000 over three years to endorse a small table); a cue deal with E J Riley Ltd; a £25,000 a year column for the *Daily Star;* personal appearances for Coral Racing and John Courage (this was worth over £220,000 for three years). Besides Davis could command £1500 for an exhibition and he jetted all over the world in a hectic round of engagements.

His successes in the 1981–2 season included the Benson and Hedges masters, the Tolly Cobbold classic, the Yamaha Organs, the Pontins festival and BBC's *Pot Black*. In 1982–3 he gradually worked his way back to his all-conquering best form — winning the Lada classic, the Hofmeister world doubles with Tony Meo, the Benson and Hedges Irish masters, the Tolly Cobbold and the Langs whisky tournament. He retained the *Pot Black* title in that superb final against Reardon and he was in completely the right frame of mind for the world championships at the Crucible, Sheffield. He beat Rex Williams, Dennis Taylor and Eddie Charlton for a semi-final place against Alex Higgins, the defending champion.

Davis was always in control of the 'Hurricane' and won 16–5 with cruelly consistent potting. In the final he had an unexpectedly easy passage against Cliff Thorburn, who was exhausted after a series of long matches and deflated by news from Canada that his wife had had a miscarriage. Davis col-

lected £30,000 from his 18—6 victory — which makes an interesting comparison with Reardon's £1500 pay day in 1973 and shows how snooker has grown under the influence of television.

He put his new-found form down to his father, Bill, and to Frank Callan, who is a fishmonger in Blackpool and helped Davis plan both world championship wins. Barry Hearn estimated that Davis could expect to earn £¾m in 1983/4 from tournaments and endorsements.

Prize money for 1982–83
Individual

Langs Scottish masters (winner;	£9,000
Jameson international	£2,500
Professional players' tournament (did not take part)	—
Coral UK championship	£2,000
Lada classic (winner)	£16,000
Benson & Hedges masters	£2,500
Tolly Cobbold (winner)	£5,000
Yamaha international masters	£2,800
Benson and Hedges Irish masters (winner)	£10,680
Embassy world championship (winner)	£30,000
	£80,480

Team

State Express world team championship (runners-up, England)	£3,500
	(share of £10,500)
Hofmeister Lager world doubles (winner with Tony Meo)	£12,000
	(share of £24,000)
Highest break	£1,000
	(share of £2,000)
Total	£96,980

Steve Davis
The king is dead, long live the king. Steve Davis shakes hands with Alex Higgins after his crushing win in the semi-final of the 1983 world championship. This defeat cost Higgins his title which Davis went on to claim by beating Cliff Thorburn for a £30,000 first prize.

The Stars/5

Alex Higgins

Nicknamed 'The Hurricane' for his fast potting style, Higgins won two world titles, ten years apart. Born on 18 March 1949 he learned to play the game in a Belfast hall called the Jampot and won the Irish amateur title. A one-time stable lad in Berkshire, he was very much an outsider in the 1972 world championships and had to survive the qualifying rounds. That he did, quite comfortably, before going on to topple some of the game's biggest names of the time — John Pulman, Rex Williams and in the final John Spencer, the holder — spoke volumes for his prodigious natural talent.

Snooker's rapid rise in popularity coincided neatly with Alex Higgins' emergence on the world scene. Temperamental, brilliant and skilful he has always been a controversial, if somewhat erratic, character. On his day, he is simply unbeatable but on off days he can be a total disappointment. One of his darkest hours was when he conceded the world final to Reardon in 1976 in a manner which was against the rules.

Higgins again lost the 1980 world final to Cliff Thorburn, but found his form superbly to win the 1982 world title, beating Ray Reardon in the final. That tearful victory was something of a triumph for the Ulsterman, although many considered he should have won many more world titles with his great talent.

A flamboyant character, something is always happening when Higgins is playing. He commands great fees as the leading exhibition player on the circuit although his enigmatic behaviour has not always been welcomed by sponsors and officials. If anyone doubts his nickname, the Hurricane once made a break of fifty in three minutes.

His wife Lynn (28) and his daughter, Lauren, born in December 1980, have brought him stability. Higgins admitted after the birth of his daughter: 'Maybe I'm getting a little mellow — a daughter can do that to you. If I'm away out of town now, instead of having another drink, I go and buy her some clothes.' He won many new friends after his emotional 1982 world championship success when Lauren seemed as important to him as the trophy.

The Hurricane's social scene is much quieter these days. Instead of sipping vodka into the small hours, he hurries home to Manchester, often by private plane. Yet controversy is always around the corner when Higgins is playing. In the 1983 world championships he was involved in a row with an opponent (Thorne) and with the referee (in his quarter final against Werbeniuk) before being thrashed 16–5 by Steve Davis in the semi-final.

The Stars/6

Terry Griffiths

This Welshman went straight to the top early in his professional career by winning the 1979 world title. That victory underlined his great ability but he has not always flourished in the years after that outstanding success.

He was Benson & Hedges masters champion in 1980 and won the Lada classic in 1982. But apart from those wins and a hat-trick in the Benson & Hedges Irish masters championship (1980–2) he has slipped from the summit. His consolation was to win the 1982 UK title for the first time when he beat Higgins 16–15 in the final at Preston.

Griffiths, from Llanelli, Dyfed, is a quiet, friendly man who even on television can be seen humming to himself and giving himself little lectures. He seems relaxed and easy going but friends will tell you that Griffiths possesses a strong, driving streak and that he is full of gut determination. He even wants to win practice matches against friends.

Born on 16 October 1947, he was formerly a bus conductor, postman and insurance salesman before becoming a professional snooker player. His favourite relaxation is watching Wales play rugby. He began playing snooker at fourteen and as an amateur won the West Wales championship at seventeen. He made his first century break at twenty-four.

In 1975, he won the Welsh amateur title and in 1976 was a beaten quarter-finalist in the world amateur; he won the All-England title that year and in 1977. Griffiths turned professional in 1978 when he was 31 (late by present standards). With characteristic modesty he explains his success: 'Concentration is everything, especially in still-ball games.'

He was a member of the successful Welsh team in the 1980 world cup. He was surprisingly beaten in the first round of the 1982 world championships by Willie Thorne and, because of his poor patch in the early 1980s, dropped to fourteenth in the world rankings for a time. In the 1983 world championship Griffiths lost 12–13 to Cliff Thorburn in the quarter final. He had pulled back from 9–12 down only to lose the deciding frame in a long and epic battle between the two most remorselessly steady players in the game. Anyway his great skills, courage and courtesy make him a superb ambassador for his sport.

Tony Knowles

Knowles will always be remembered as the man who so sensationally put out the defending champion, Steve Davis, in the first round of the 1982 world championships, by ten frames to one. Knowles, from Bolton, is a former British junior champion but has not yet made the complete transition from that level to the top of the professional ranks.

A good player, so far he has lacked the consistency of potting and total concentration required for success at the highest professional standard.

There were signs of growing maturity in the 1983 world championships when he beat Tony Meo before losing to Steve Davis in the semi-finals.

He turned professional in 1980 and was a member of the England team in the 1982 team classic. His first major tournament victory came in the 1982 Jameson International when he beat David Taylor in the final, giving him his highest pay cheque of £22,000. Born on 13 June 1955, Knowles started playing snooker at nine years of age.

Tony Knowles

Terry Griffiths

Jimmy White

White was denied his first professional tournament win in England when Ray Reardon beat him in the final of the 1982 tournament players' final and again in the 1983 Yamaha Organs masters. But his progress to that final illustrated that he was gaining the vital experience required to win at the top. He disappointed in the 1983 world championships, losing in the first round to Tony Meo.

Born in 1962, he comes from the London suburb of Tooting and gained a reputation as a brilliant, but erratic — often wild — player. Safe, defensive play is totally alien to his nature although his appearance in the Yamaha final proved he was adding those characteristics to his game.

He went to the same school as Tony Meo, another promising young London player, and he made his first century break when he was only thirteen. The possessor of a great natural talent, he will surely win many trophies if he settles himself rather more and understands the need for patience and composure at the table. Defence, too, is a part of the game he needs to add to his repertoire.

A former winner of the British Boys championship, he became the youngest player to capture the English amateur title at sixteen. He also won the world amateur championship in 1980 in Tasmania. His first big professional win came in the 1981 Langs Scottish masters tournament in Glasgow when he beat Cliff Thorburn. He also won the Northern Ireland classic, beating Steve Davis 11–9 in the final.

Cliff Thorburn

Thorburn shocked snooker by winning the 1980 world title, beating Alex Higgins in the final to earn a £15,000 cheque. But this popular Canadian — who was born in Ontario on 16 January 1948 — suffered a crisis in his career as soon as he had achieved his greatest ambition.

His decision to move to England to live after that world title success was a mistake which badly affected his game. He and his family did not settle in their Surrey home and Thorburn's form deteriorated. Things did not improve significantly until the family moved back to Canada and restored their traditional roots. Then as if to show his satisfaction, Thorburn won the 1983 Benson & Hedges masters at Wembley — his first big success since the world title win.

In the 1983 world championships, Thorburn experienced triumph and tribulation in finishing runner-up to Steve Davis. The triumph was his maximum break against Terry Griffiths — the first in the history of the event. Thorburn began the break with a fluke on a red after Griffiths had fouled on the white. As tension mounted the players on the other table stopped to watch and, with compatriot Bill Werbeniuk looking on, Thorburn sank to his knees as the last black disappeared.

Thorburn overcame Griffiths after a titantic struggle and was forced into another cliffhanger against Tony Knowles in the semi-final. In the middle of this match he heard that his wife Barbara had suffered a miscarriage and he was drained for the final against Davis. 'I now know what purgatory is like,' he said afterwards. But he still collected £28,000 for his pains — £15,000 as runner up, £10,000 for the maximum break and £3,000 for the highest break of the tournament.

A former champion of North America and Canada, he first appeared on the English snooker scene in 1973. He won the 1974 Australian masters tournament and steadily improved as a player on the world stage. He reached the final of the 1977 world professional championship, only to lose to John Spencer after a close battle. He also won the 1981 BBC *Pot Black* title.

Cliff Thorburn's maximum

The Embassy world championships will be remembered mainly for the magical 147 by Canada's Cliff Thorburn in the quarter final against Terry Griffiths. Thorburn became the first player to achieve a maximum in the world championships and this unique record can never be broken (only equalled).

But this great break started on a strange note. First Griffiths committed a foul early in the frame when he failed to make contact with a red in attempting a safety shot. Thorburn came to the table to find the balls nicely spread, but his first scoring pot was a fluke—a red rebounded from the jaws of the top righthand pocket, ran along the top cushion and sent another red trickling into the top lefthand pocket (fig 1).

They all count and Thorburn grimaced at this stroke of good fortune before mopping up. In sinking his fifteen reds and fifteen blacks he was rarely out of position or in trouble.

His most testing moments came when he was nearing that magic maximum. His positional play with the cue ball was excellent in setting up the last red/black combination (fig 2), but he left himself some distance from the yellow when he came to tackle the remaining colours (fig 3). However, an excellent pot across the table kept the break going and he worked his way inexorably to the final black (fig 4).

As Thorburn lined up that last black, commentator Jack Karnehm showed that he was as nervous as anyone in the Crucible Theatre or watching at home on television. 'Good luck, mate' Karnehm whispered with a tremor in his voice.

Nothing could stop the former world champion now and as the last black disappeared he fell to his knees beside the table with his arms aloft in triumph. His compatriot, Bill Werbeniuk, had stopped playing on the adjoining table to watch the climax and now he joined Griffiths in a triple hug of celebration with the ecstatic Thorburn.

This was the first display of emotion by the steely Thorburn—although when his score had reached 105 he did break off to blow his nose and towel down his hands and cue. The maximum earned Thorburn £13,000—which was made up of £10,000 for the 147 itself and £3,000 for the highest break of the tournament. A great night's work!

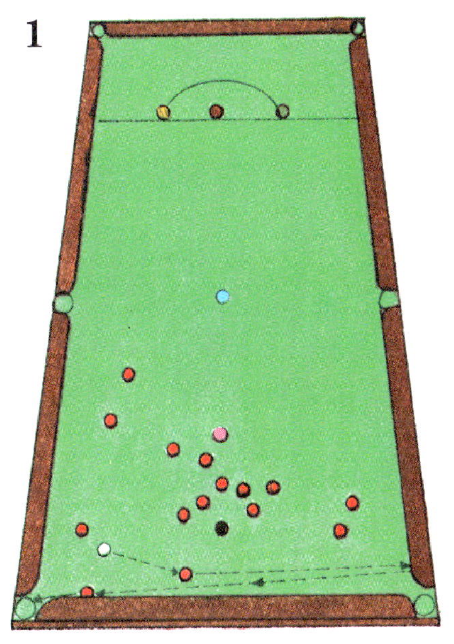

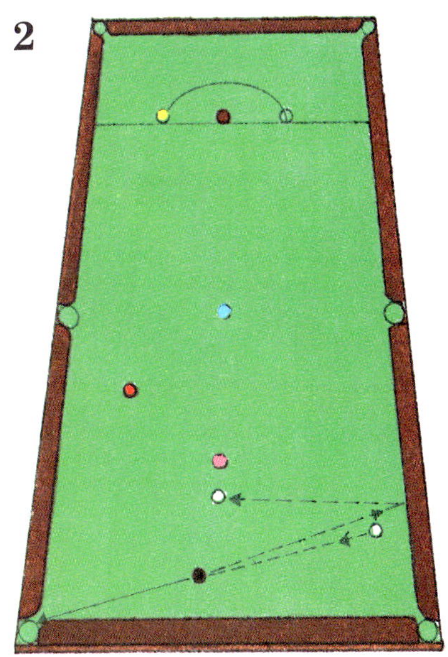

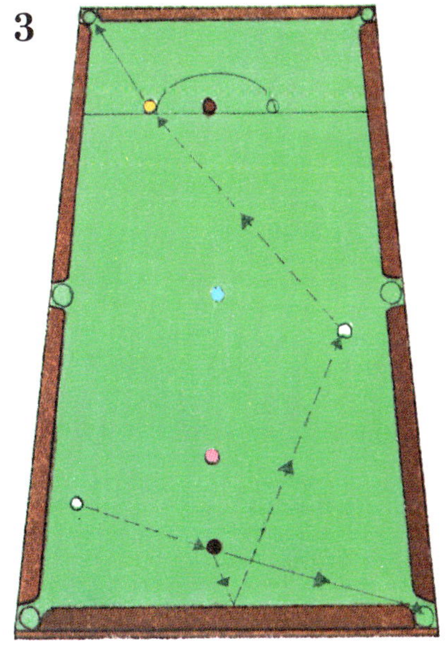

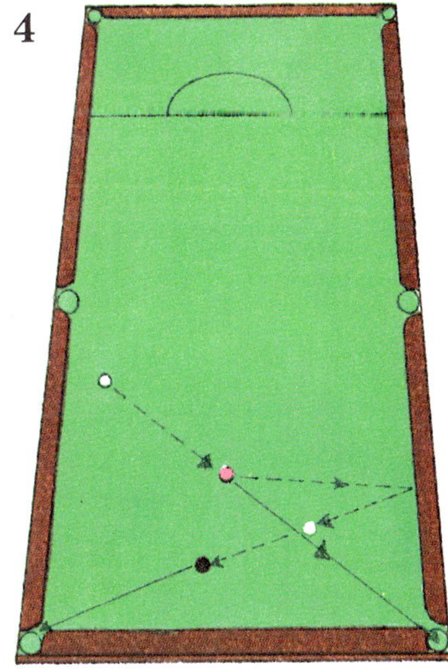

Tony Meo
Born in London in 1959, the son of Italian parents, he became the 1978 junior champion at the age of nineteen. But it was his form in the Canadian open championships that year which marked him as a player of potential. He reached the final of that tournament, beating, among others, Alex Higgins.

He lost to Cliff Thorburn in that final but since then has proved that early flourish was no freak. He is managed by Barry Hearn, the promoter who also guides Steve Davis and Terry Griffiths. He has made high breaks throughout his short career including a maximum 147 at the age of seventeen — the youngest player ever to achieve that feat.

In the 1983 world championships he showed more signs of progress, beating White and Mountjoy before losing to Knowles in the quarter-finals. Earlier that season he won the Hofmeister doubles with Steve Davis.

Tony Meo

Willie Thorne

Born in 1955, Thorne lives in Leicester and is regarded as one of snooker's up-and-coming young players. He caused a sensation in the 1982 world championships by beating the new favourite Terry Griffiths in round one (after Steve Davis had also lost in the first round). He went on to beat John Spencer but lost to the eventual champion, Alex Higgins, in the quarter-finals.

Thorne has made more 147 maximum breaks than any other player — 29 in all. In the 1982 match against Higgins he made a 143 break.

He now runs a snooker centre in Leicester but needs to earn a major title to make the real breakthrough. He won the 1980 Pontins festival at Prestatyn defeating, among others, Steve Davis.

Willie Thorne

Bill Werbeniuk

Born in 1947 at Winnipeg in Canada's Manitoba province, he was based in Vancouver, but in recent years has spent most of his time playing the game in Britain. He paid £20,000 for a bus to be converted, enabling him to tour Britain playing tournaments without incurring excessive hotel expenses!

A popular, jocular character, his 18st bulk makes him easily recognisable as the heftiest player on the British circuit. He was a losing quarter-finalist in the world professional championships of 1978, 1979 and 1981, picking up the tag of 'the nearly man' which he has yet to lose.

The closest he came to a major success in Britain was in the 1983 Lada classic when, playing some of the most consistent snooker of his career, he reached the final before losing 9–5 to Steve Davis, having beaten Alex Higgins, Doug Mountjoy and Kirk Stevens.

Nerves have always been a problem for him and he has become accustomed to consuming a large amount of lager to settle him before major matches. The cure' has helped his game perhaps — but not his figure!

Graham Miles

His victory in the 1981 Tolly Cobbold classic was the first for this Birmingham-based player since his halcyon days of the mid-1970s. Then, he finished runner-up to Ray Reardon in the 1974 world final and won the BBC *Pot Black* title in 1974 and 1975, as well as being runner-up to Doug Mountjoy in the 1978 competition.

At his best, he has beaten just about every big-name snooker star in the world. But lack of consistency in recent years has impeded his progress and he has slipped back to around twentieth in the world rankings. He was born on 11 April 1941.

Doug Mountjoy

His best tournament, by far, was the 1981 world professional championships at Sheffield where he reached the final before losing 18 frames to 12 to Steve Davis. But to reach that final, he had beaten Willie Thorne, Eddie Charlton, Dennis Taylor and Ray Reardon and had also made the highest break of the tournament, 145 against Reardon in the all-Welsh semi-final. It was also the record break in the history of the world championships, an achievement which earned him £5,000 in addition to the £1,200 biggest break prize — and the runner-up prize of £10,000 — a total of £16,200 for his work at that tournament. He has now lost that record to Thorburn.

He comes from Ebbw Vale, born on 8 June 1942, and is a past winner of the Welsh professional title. In fact, he won that title twice in three years, which was a great achievement considering the quality of other eligible players such as Ray Reardon and Terry Griffiths.

In 1980, he won the Champion of Champions title and then helped Griffiths and Reardon steer Wales to the State Express world cup for the second consecutive year. He was *Pot Black* champion in 1978 and runner-up in 1977 and 1979. A former miner, he is a steady, consistent potter and can beat the best players in the world, as he has proved on several occasions.

Cliff Wilson

A long-standing adversary of Ray Reardon who also comes from Tredegar, Wilson was born in 1935 and is now approaching the veteran stage among all the youngsters on the professional circuit! He made a most promising start to his snooker career and was twice British junior champion. But problems with his eyesight forced him to retire from the game for many years, thus robbing the immensely talented Wilson of valuable years' experience in the amateur ranks.

He did not start playing again seriously until the mid-1970s and he did not turn professional until the age of forty-four. By then, he had won Welsh amateur titles in 1977 and 1979, as well as the world amateur title in Malta in 1978. The closest he came to a professional success was when he lost to Ray Reardon in the final of the 1981 Welsh professional championship.

Kirk Stevens

Stevens is a flamboyant, exciting young Canadian player who has been a regular on the British professional circuit for a few years now. He comes from Toronto where he was born on 17 August 1958 and has been a member of the Canadian side in the State Express team competitions of recent years.

He won the Canadian championship in 1979, beating Cliff Thorburn in the final. By then, he was just twenty-one, underlining the great talent at his disposal. A year earlier, he had lost to the Welshman Cliff Wilson in the semi-finals of the world amateur championship in Malta.

He provided quite a few shocks — and glimpses of his immense ability — by reaching the semi-finals of the 1980 world professional championship before losing to Higgins. In 1982, he reached the quarter-finals of the world championships before losing to White. In the 1983 event, he went out 13–12 to Thorburn at the same stage. But his fine displays in the early 1980s gave him a prominent ranking in the first ten of the world's top players.

He first played snooker at the age of ten in the Golden Cue Centre, Scarboro, Toronto. But like Cliff Thorburn and Bill Werbeniuk, Kirk has had to move to Britain to further his career because Canadian snooker is not far enough advanced to offer the professional player a good livelihood.

David Taylor

This Manchester-based professional came close to his first major tournament win when he lost the final of the 1982 Jameson international to Tony Knowles. He was a fine amateur player, winning both the English and world championships in the same year, 1968.

He turned professional later that year but it was ten years before he contested a major final, losing the UK professional championship to Doug Mountjoy. He did well in the 1980 world professional championship, reaching the semi-finals before losing to the eventual winner, Thorburn.

He also lost to Thorburn, his bogey opponent, in the 1981 event, at the quarter-final stage. That year he was runner-up to Steve Davis in the Yamaha Organs international masters but 1982 saw him finish on the winning side, being a member of the successful English team in the world team classic. Taylor is easily recognisable with his silver hair, but he has yet to succeed in making the difficult transition from good pro player to tournament winner. He was born on 29 July 1943.

Jim Wych

Another of the fine young Canadian professionals who are having an increasing impact on the British scene, Wych was born in Calgary, Alberta, in 1955. He is a former Canadian amateur champion and turned professional in 1980, the year after his amateur success, following his fellow countrymen like Thorburn, Werbeniuk and Stevens to Britain.

He made a marvellous start in the professional ranks, reaching the final of the 1980 Canadian championship before losing to Thorburn. He also made an audacious beginning in the *Pot Black* tournament, finishing as runner-up in the 1981 event (again seeing Thorburn lift the trophy as winner).

A left-hander, he has not quite lived up to that good start to his professional life but has the ability to develop as a fine player for the future and become a tournament winner. According to Wych, Canadian opinion of snooker was so poor that he did not like to be seen carrying a cue in his home town.

John Virgo

A player of great class, it is surprising that he has failed to achieve regular tournament success. Lack of concentration is generally regarded as the reason, for on his day he is more than capable of beating any player in the world. He is very popular on the exhibition circuit for his light-hearted impressions of many of his fellow players.

He was born in Lancashire in 1946 and turned professional at the age of thirty after winning several amateur titles. He lost to Dennis Taylor in the semi-finals of the 1979 world professional championship — the closest he has ever been to an appearance on professional snooker's greatest stage.

But he has won events such as the 1979 Coral UK professional championship and also won a tournament in Bombay later that same year. He won the 1980 Pontin's professional tournament but since then has been struggling to land the major trophies.

Road to the top/1

For the leading players of the 1980s, the need for constant practice has become an ingrained habit. Any player appearing before the television cameras will have spent years perfecting the art and technique of the game. Snooker demands extensive practice to reach the top level and to stay there, even for established players like Alex Higgins, Ray Reardon and Steve Davis.

Snooker requires the unusual combination of a calm temperament and a killer instinct. It is a game in which it is absolutely essential to take advantage of an opponent's errors, because frames are won by players who prolong their visits to the table and build up breaks.

Leading players know they may get only one or two chances of building a commanding score during a game. If you are playing an opponent who is on a hot streak and you make an error to let him in, you face a long wait in your chair. In that sense, snooker can be a defensive game and it is important not to leave an opponent any easy pots.

At the same time, you must take advantage of an opponent's errors. The player who lets an opponent off from a mistake will not go far. Snooker at the highest level is all about seizing the initiative or denying it until the right chance arrives and capitalising on your opportunities when they occur. If you miss one chance, you may not get another and that frame could go out of the window, so to speak.

Nowadays, the top players are regular performers under the television cameras and lights. They must learn to conquer their nerves and overcome the inevitable tension in front of an audience of millions. Armchair critics may be at a loss to understand how the best players in the world can miss straightforward shots which look a formality. But they do not take into account the atmosphere, the tension

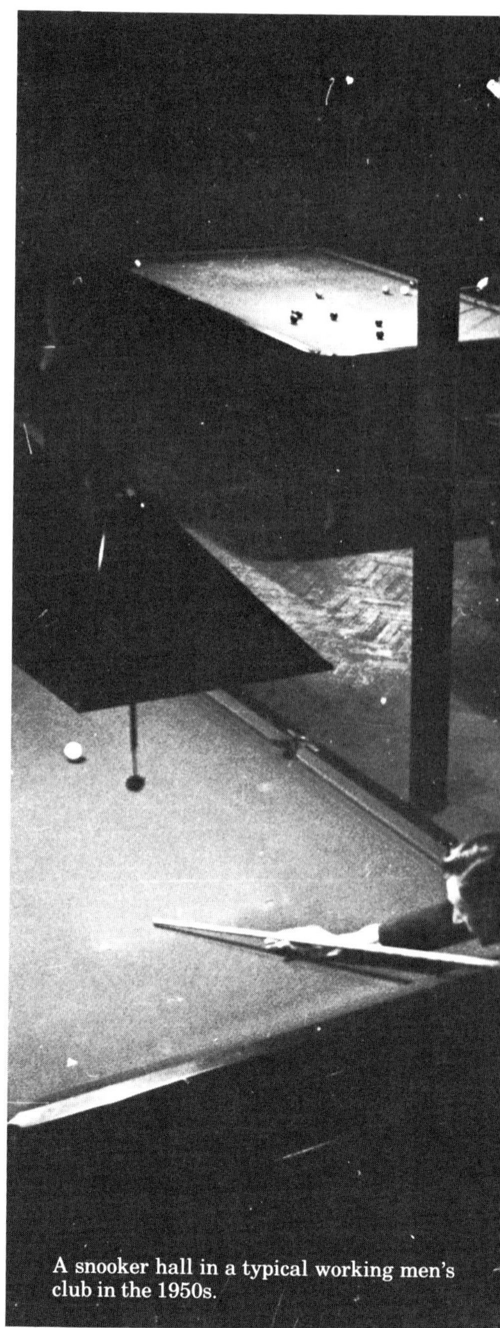

A snooker hall in a typical working men's club in the 1950s.

and the anxiety which the TV cameras and lights bring to bear.

Most of our leading players probably began playing by the time they were ten or twelve and thereafter steadily improved through competition at junior level. County competitions follow, with the select few standing out at that stage. Only the very best will emerge — those players able to cope with the pressure of big time competitions.

Sacrifice is essential, as is the case in every sport. Hour after hour spent on the practice table is the only answer. Alex Higgins, for instance, spent every available moment at a table in the Jampot, Belfast, and from the age of twelve challenged (and beat) older opponents there and at the Belfast YMCA.

Snooker may seem a glittering and extremely lucrative occupation for apparently little effort. But in reality its leading exponents will have trodden a familiar treadmill. Taking part in tournaments from an early age is especially important. There are, without doubt, some fine players outside the professional ranks, players who seem to have the talent to progress to the higher echelons of the game. Without the ability to take competition — and all its inherent stresses in your stride — you can expect little success.

Top players insist that after years of competition, even at junior level, they still feel nervous on the big occasions. Despite all the experience gained in matchplay, they are still susceptible to the demands of competition. They will stress to any budding young hopeful the need for competition from an early age.

After tackling opponents of amateur standing — who have, not in a derogatory sense, an amateur attitude and approach — the new professional finds himself pitted against the finest players in the world. He must improve and adapt his game to cope with a greater challenge. He must also learn to look ahead and think through a situation.

By mastering the techniques of screw shots and stuns, the player can position the cue-ball where he requires it to be for the next shot. By doing this a player can make his life considerably easier. Having to produce brilliant shots full of side, screw or stun merely to get the ball into the proper place for the next shot is wasting energy, physical and mental. Nor is it any use making a brilliant pot across the table and leaving nothing 'on' for the next shot.

On the road: Terry Griffiths in a hotel room prepares to enter the arena.

Events/1

The world professional championships, held each spring in England, are the climax of the snooker season. Winning the world title is the ambition of every sportsman and it is no different for the snooker player.

These days, with huge publicity and exposure on television, the commercial rewards for the successful players are greater than the prize for winning the world title. But in prestige terms, the tournament — sponsored in recent years by Embassy — is the pinnacle of all the year's events.

Other events, however, offer good prizes and enable the top players to earn a handsome living from the sport. Events such as the Yamaha Organs international masters, the Jameson's international, the Lada classic, the Hofmeister world doubles and the Woodpecker Welsh professional title illustrate the extent to which big business has become involved in the sponsorship of major snooker tournaments.

Indeed, maintaining a balance and avoiding over-exposure on television is now the major problem facing the men who govern the game in the United Kingdom. Of course, it says much for snooker's image to have had so many sponsored events available in years in recession.

While sports such as soccer struggle to attract sufficient sponsors — partly because of questions about the game's deteriorating image — sponsors queue up to plough money into snooker. They can be certain that their product will endorsed by clean-cut, well-behaved, well-dressed men, who are unlikely to tarnish the game's splendid image.

The list of tournaments with well-known sponsoring companies spreads throughout the snooker calendar. Others, besides those mentioned already, include the Benson & Hedges masters, the Coral UK championships and the Langs Supreme Scottish

On the world stage: Alex Higgins (left) and Bill Werbeniuk wait for battle to continue in the 1983 world championships.

masters. They are by no means all and still more are in the pipeline for future promotions. It is a story of unrivalled success for attracting promotional business.

Not all the snooker tournaments, are major events for professionals. Competitions are held right through the range of playing capability, professional and amateur. County tournaments flourish; there are inter-county competitions and local leagues featuring the many clubs which are growing rapidly all over the country.

Prize money for the senior professionals is most attractive. For instance, the 1983 Embassy world championships had £135,000 in prize money and the Hofmeister doubles tournament, a comparatively new event, offered total prize money of £66,000 for 1983, with the winning pair sharing £24,000. Fair reward, you could say, for doing half a job! The Yamaha Organs international masters carries £55,000 prize money.

As in darts, snooker players can supplement their tournament winnings by exhibitions throughout the year. The best fees for exhibition work are paid to only the most successful snooker players.

Recent world champions — such as Steve Davis, Cliff Thorburn, Alex Higgins and Terry Griffiths — take home far more from the commercial field than money won at the events themselves. Even the money to be earned from the coveted world title seems mere petty cash in comparison with the huge sums offered for endorsement of products.

The life of the professional snooker circuit is no straightforward affair. To survive such arduous travelling and having to work at the end of each journey is not everyone's idyllic lifestyle. Many simply do not have the stamina for such a demanding schedule.

If snooker exhibitions appear to be rather less frequent than in other sports such as darts, it is because there are more tournaments arranged. Tournaments are often a form of exhibition at halls or clubs. Pontins, Butlins, Warners and other big holi-

One of the many sponsors who are queuing up to back snooker get a prominent billing as Terry Griffiths works out the angles.

day companies, for instance, arrange special promotions involving challenge matches between some of the stars. These are really exhibitions although the competitive flavour is increased by the number of star players attracted.

So the snooker world is filled with a whole series of events and competitions, big and small, for amateur and professional. The game is clearly a most competitive animal!

Venues

The growing popularity of snooker has led to a mushrooming of venues all over the snooker-playing world. Australia and Canada report the creation in large numbers of clubs where amateurs can enjoy a game or where top class professional tournaments can be staged.

Size is the greatest consideration. At major professional events two matches are often played simultaneously with a partition down the middle of the arena. The players, in fact, do not welcome such an arrangement because of the obvious distractions of crowd noise and reaction to the other game. But major professional events have a great many frames to play and so it is often necessary to arrange a tournament in this way, certainly in the early stages, to prevent it from being too drawn out and going on for weeks on end.

The Crucible Theatre, Sheffield, houses the world championship. But if the Crucible has become known as the mecca of world snooker, there are a great many other halls, clubs and theatres where major tournaments are staged.

The Assembly Rooms, Derby, stages the £55,000 Yamaha Organs international masters; the Spectrum Arena, Warrington, was the setting for the 1983 Lada classic. Other venues well known in the professionals' diaries are the Hexagon, Reading; the Sheffield Snooker Centre; the Romily Forum and the Crystal Palace Centre.

The Crucible theatre, Sheffield

The Yamaha Organs trophy is held aloft
by Ray Reardon, the 1983 winner.

Apart from major venues, towns such as Preston, Ebbw Vale, Bristol, Nottingham, Sunderland, Bingham (Notts), Larne (Northern Ireland), Lincoln, Mansfield, Chesterfield and Newark all stage tournaments for both amateur and professional players. Snooker is booming in more ways than one. Clubs with plush facilities have opened up everywhere to cater for a demand which has been encouraged by regular television coverage.

Membership fees vary enormously according to the facilities and number of tables. To encourage new members and create interest, many clubs hire well-known professionals to play exhibitions at their premises, thus ensuring the snooker boom maintains its momentum. Of course, the creation of all these new centres means that the game is becoming more widely available.

With full-size snooker tables costing anything from £2,500 few people can afford to buy their own. Thus, without the facilities offered by clubs, many ordinary amateur enthusiasts would only be able to play the game on rare occasions.

Snooker halls are opening in Canada, Australia and New Zealand. All over the world, the game is making rapid strides — and the vast number of new halls and leisure centres is an obvious indication of a flourishing game.

Name of the game: sponsors seek and get exposure on television and in newspapers by having their name prominently displayed. In this case it is the Benson and Hedges Masters at the Wembley conference centre and the Yamaha Organs trophy at the Assembly Rooms, Derby (with David Taylor at the table).

Equipment/1

Tables

Matches of any official or professional status are played on full-size tables measuring 12ft long, 6ft wide and just under 3ft high. The bed of the table will be made of slate, although wood and iron were used in earlier times.

Slate is a pliable material, which is easy to cut and fit to the size required and if slight damage occurs it can be repaired easily. Normal thickness of the slate is approximately 2in, although when slate beds were first introduced in the middle of the nineteenth century they were thinner than that. Slate is weighty and with wooden surround — often a strong solid wood like oak or mahogany — a snooker table is an extremely heavy object.

The development of the table has followed a predictable, sedate course over the years. Major innovations have been restricted by the nature of the object and modern tables — covered in the traditional green baize — do not differ much from those of long ago. The green baize is ironed regularly to eliminate marks and poor patches.

Cues

The advent of the leather tip greatly changed the shape and effectiveness of the cues. The tip was introduced to give a greater grip on the ball, together with the chalk applied before each shot is made.

Cues used to be known as 'maces' when the ball was pushed rather than struck. Finally, with the coming of the modern cue-tip, the mace end disappeared, although it bore a likeness to the flat end on the butt of the cue.

Most cues, or at least the best ones, are made of ash or maple. But preparation of the wood is essential to prevent warping or bending at a later date.

Cues vary in length but the ideal size is probably one which reaches a height just below the player's shoulder. However, professional players have cues of varying lengths and it is a matter of personal preference as to what length is most comfortable for the individual concerned.

Weights also range from the light — about 12 oz — to the comparatively heavy at over 22oz. The best weight, lies between the two — moderation in all things, in other words. The cue should be finished to a perfect, smooth

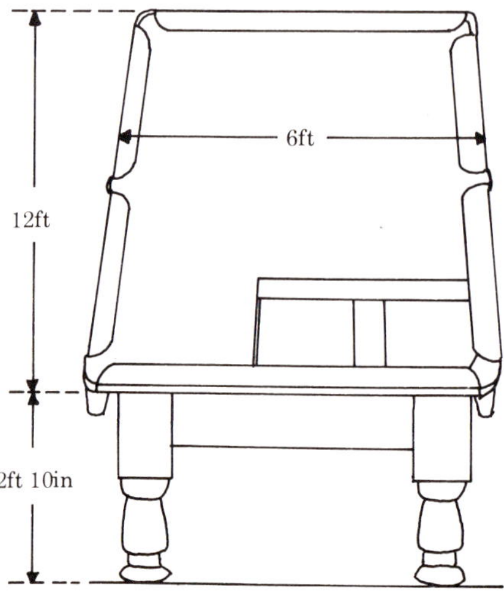

surface, thus allowing a comfortable sliding movement through the bridge made by the hand, before striking the ball.

Tips

Tips should be rounded in design, almost dome-like in appearance and *always* covered in chalk before a shot. If you wonder why all the professional players take such meticulous care to chalk their tips before every shot, it is because the tip is one of the most important aspects in the game.

If the tip is covered unevenly with chalk or, worse still, without a sufficient covering, the possibility of a miscue is considerably increased. Chalk ensures a good, clean contact between the cue's leather tip — the gripping part — and the ball.

In fact, top professionals spend almost more time in selecting and getting the feel of their ideal tips than on any other piece of equipment. It is often a question of feel because some tips are soft, pliable and almost too yielding; others are too hard and therefore make an uncomfortable contact with the ball.

The importance of a perfect tip is illustrated by the playing of the side, stun, screw or swerve shots. Striking the ball at an angle, perhaps on the bottom or on one side, requires firm yet proper contact. A tip which slides off a ball, because it is not making the right contact exactly in the middle is no use to professional players attempting difficult shots and seeking to get the cue-ball in position.

So players take great care of the cues and especially tips. Repairs should be done only after consultation with experts and harsh materials should never be used to rectify a fault. Remember, the tip is made of leather and is soft. Using hard materials on it will damage it permanently.

Equipment/2

Rests

In tournaments rests are provided with each table and are the responsibility of the promoting company. Every kind of rest is available for the senior players, from the basic 5ft rest to the longer ones, which can be 7 or 9ft long. For those rests, you will need to use a special long cue, which must always be chalked thoroughly before use. It is more than likely that the long cue-tip will need attention, because it is not used very often. Careful scrutiny of this special cue should be made before attempting any shot with the aid of the rest.

If a shot has to be played in a difficult position some distance from the player, a rest will be required. It is always much better to use the rest than crawl halfway across the table with your body uncomfortable and badly positioned (and if you do you must still have the statutory one foot on the floor). Do not be lazy and not bother to get out the rest. It is a part of the game which should become, in time, as natural as any other, although it does cause a great many players considerable problems.

If a shot has to be played with the cue-ball near another ball, the spider may be needed. This form of rest provides a higher platform from which to strike the cue ball, thus gaining an aerial position from which to make contact. The greatest danger with a spider is touching a nearby ball before you have made contact with your intended shot. Place the spider with great care and keep a firm grip on it. If you let it slip, it can touch a ball and cost you a penalty.

The art of using a rest is shown by the restless Alex Higgins.

Clothing

No special clothing is required in the ordinary sense for the game of snooker. But if there is one important exception to that rule it would be the footwear.

Shoes with slippery soles would be a great disadvantage for a snooker player who often has to balance himself on one foot. So make sure your shoes have good grip and in competitions, you may be required to wear a smart outfit.

Expensive suits are not necessary but a shirt and something around the neck like a bow-tie. An ordinary tie might fall onto the table and be an encumbrance. If professionals wear a normal tie, they usually put on a waistcoat. Some players, like Alex Higgins, prefer not to wear anything around the neck. But a recent ruling by snooker's governing body at the professional level insisted that a player must wear a neck-piece. Higgins has had to accept the ruling athough he and Cliff Wilson have doctors' certificates which allow them to remove their ties at certain times.

The top professionals take almost as much care with their clothing and general appearance as with their snooker equipment. Long, untidy hair would not only look bad but be a nuisance to a player who must concentrate without interruption on the shot he is attempting. Sponsors, like players to look smart, because that helps to promote the clean-cut image of the game and aids the selling of products.

Stripping for action: Higgins unbuttons his tie before doing battle with Bill Werbeniuk.

Equipment/3

Balls

The original billiard balls were made of ivory, which was imported into the United Kingdom in great quantities in the late nineteenth century. As it became a prohibitively costly material, requiring the slaughter of elephants, new materials were sought.

In the 1860s, celluloid balls were introduced and in 1900, the crystalate ball, a composition ball with a base of cellulose nitrate. This was later accepted as the standard ball. Cast resin balls with a base of phenol and formaldehyde — called Vitalite — were also invented.

Prices

A full-size snooker table (or to give it its correct name, billiards table) has a playing surface of 12ft long by 6ft wide with a height of approximately 2ft 10in. The Italian slate bed is supported by a wooden frame and legs usually of mahogany, oak or walnut. The slate slabs composing the bed are 1½–2in thick and the whole table weighs about 1¾ tons.

It takes craftsmen to build these tables with the best materials and the cost of full-size tables is therefore high — from £2,250 to £5,000 for a championship table.

Smaller tables are available and are

Ready to go: a full set of 15 reds, 1 black, 1 pink, 1 blue, 1 brown, 1 green, 1 yellow and the white cue-ball ... and the triangle is removed from the pack of reds before the start of a frame.

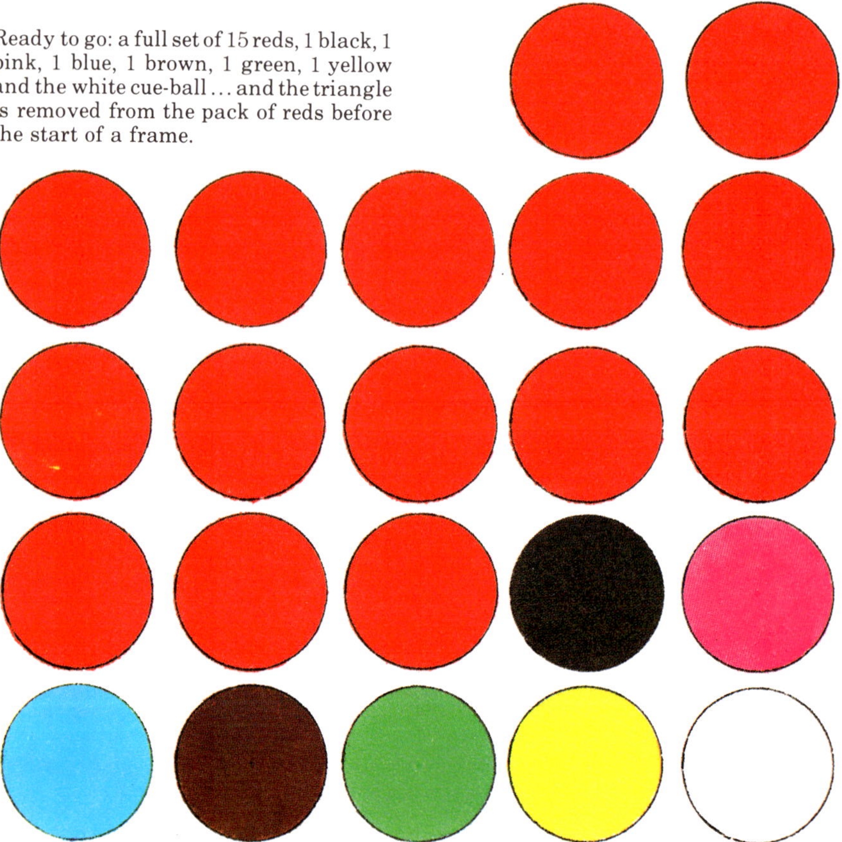

useful for practice. Budget tables range from £90–£200 for the half-size, 6ft by 3ft, with more expensive models in this size from £200–£600, with slate beds and optional dining tops.

The cue is vital to a snooker player, as we have said, and Steve Davis has remarked that he would rather lose his Porsche than his cue! The cue is made from wood, the best from ash but other woods can be used and Canadian maple is popular, especially in North America and for the cheaper cues.

Full-size cues (4ft 10in) can be bought for between £10 and £16 for the beginner, with top class cues topping £80. Until 1970, one-piece cues were the norm but since then, the two-piece cue has been increasing in popularity. Professionals invest in top class cues, which should last many years with careful looking after. Fred Davis has been playing with the same cue for fifty years.

Miscellaneous costs	approx.
A set of snooker balls	£70.00
Extension spider rest	£17.00
Spider rest or cross rest	£7.00
Half butt rest	£9.00
Long butt with long rest	£13.00
Cue chalk (six pieces)	£0.60
Cue tipping set	£1.75
Stick-on cue tips (six)	£1.00
Table brush	£13.00
Triangle	£10.00
Snooker ball marker	£1.45

Although an amateur player needs no special clothes in which to play, the professionals need dress suits and accessories and pay £350 for a suit (the jacket usually spending more time on the hanger than on the player), up to £150 on shoes, £25–45 on a shirt, £20 on a silk tie and £5 on a silk or satin bow tie.

People in the media/1

Ted Lowe

The BBC's Ted Lowe is one of the veterans of the snooker commentators. Lowe helped found the popular BBC TV series *Pot Black* which began in 1969 and had a major hand in the rapid development of the professional game in the 1970s. *Pot Black* was an innovation and a revelation. It brought the top stars into the homes of millions and it opened up numerous commercial possibilities for the leading performers. The programme attracts 6m viewers and it has undoubtedly paved the way for snooker's TV explosion — 12m people watched the 1982 Yamaha final.

Lowe started in the business in the days of Raymond Glendenning, whom he replaced at the eleventh hour for one horse racing commentary job. One thing led to another and Lowe's passion for snooker made him the obvious choice for commentaries when snooker came to the small screen.

But Lowe had been involved in snooker a long time before *Pot Black*. He helped to set up snooker centres in London after the Second World War and he was general manager at the Leicester Square Hall until 1955 when it moved to new premises. He also helped to form the Referees' Association and the Professional Players' Association. Lowe quickly saw the need for organised bodies to direct the growing popularity of snooker and his organisational skills and understanding of the game helped enormously in those early days.

Lowe's smooth, dark tones are as popular as ever. They are the perfect balance for a game usually played before hushed audiences — the low, gravelly voice blending with the action.

Jack Karnehm (left) and Ted Lowe

Rex Williams

Another commentator of long experience is Rex Williams, who was born on 20 July 1933 and has played the game successfully throughout his adult life. Williams is still considered a fine player and no wonder because he has achieved the maximum break of 147 no less than four times in his competitive career.

He became the youngest player to win the English amateur championship at the age of seventeen in 1951 and by then had twice been boys champion at billiards and snooker.

His pedigree was established. He won the world professional billiards championship in 1968, 1971, 1973 — when he was also runner-up in BBC's *Pot Black* competition.

Williams has come close to similar honours in professional snooker. He reached the semi-finals of the 1972 world championship before losing to the eventual winner, Alex Higgins. He also lost in the semi-finals in 1974 and so never quite matched his success at snooker with his undoubted mastery of billiards.

People in the media/2

John Spencer

Another former player who can be heard from the commentary box these days is John Spencer, a former snooker world champion. Spencer, from Manchester, won the title in 1969, 1970 and 1977.

Spencer was born on 15 September 1935. When he was fifteen, he made a break of 115 but he left the game, for almost ten years because of National Service and other commitments. But Spencer possessed the ability to bridge the gap and became a prolific winner.

He is a past champion of the *Pot Black* series on two occasions.

John Pulman

John Pulman brings an unrivalled experience of playing success within the game to the commentary box. Born on 12 December 1923, Pulman, who is more than 6ft tall, won the world professional title ten times from 1958 to 1968 — when John Spencer beat him in the quarter-final on his way to the title. Pulman never won the title again although he reached the final once more, losing to Ray Reardon.

If John Spencer's achievement of a 115 break at the age of fifteen was considered special, Pulman's first billiards century break at the age of

John Spencer

The BBC commentary team (left to right): John Spencer, Jack Karnehm, Ted Lowe, Rex Williams, Clive Everton, Ray Edmonds.

twelve was even better. He won the English amateur immediately after the Second World War, in 1946, and he turned professional later that year, earning £400 in his first tournament.

He had to withstand a desperately tough baptism in the professional ranks, meeting players like Joe and Fred Davis on many occasions. But Pulman, who hails from Devon, was not deterred and his remarkable run of successes in the world championship confirmed earlier forecasts that he would become a great champion in his own right.

Dennis Taylor

The Northern Ireland player, Dennis Taylor, is also a regular broadcaster on the game, when he is not involved in tournaments himself. Taylor, who was born on 19 January 1949 and is based in Blackburn, was winning titles in the 1960s. The first of them was the British junior billiards championship in 1968.

As a player, he has perhaps not quite fulfilled early promise but he is still good enough to trouble the best in the professional game. He is popular on the circuit and from the commentary box represents the thoughts of the modern professional.

Statistics

World championships

1969	J Spencer beat G Owen, 37-24
1970 (Apr)	R Reardon beat J Pulman, 37-33
1970 (Nov)	J Spencer beat W Simpson, 37-29
1972	A Higgins beat J Spencer, 37-32
1973	R Reardon beat E Charlton, 38-32
1974	R Reardon beat G Miles, 22-12
1975	(in Australia) R Reardon beat E Charlton, 31-30
1976	R Reardon beat A Higgins, 27-16
1977	J Spencer beat C Thorburn, 25-21
1978	R Reardon beat P Mans, 25-18
1979	T Griffiths beat Dennis Taylor, 24-16
1980	C Thorburn beat A Higgins, 18-16
1981	S Davis beat D Mountjoy, 18-12
1982	A Higgins beat R Reardon, 18-15
1983	S Davis beat C Thorburn, 18-6

Sponsors: 1969, April 1970 Players No 6
November 1970, 1975 None
1972-4 Park Drive
1976- Embassy

Tolly Cobbold classic

1979	A Higgins beat R Reardon, 5-4
1980	A Higgins beat Dennis Taylor, 5-4
1981	G Miles beat C Thorburn, 5-1
1982	S Davis beat Dennis Taylor, 8-3
1983	S Davis beat T Griffiths, 7-5

Wilsons classic

1980	J Spencer beat A Higgins, 4-3
1981	S Davis beat Dennis Taylor, 4-1

Superseded by:

Lada classic

1982	T Griffiths beat S Davis, 9-8
1983	S Davis beat B Werbeniuk, 9-5

Yamaha Organs trophy

1981	S Davis beat David Taylor, 9-6
1982	S Davis beat T Griffiths, 9-7
1983	R Reardon beat J White, 9-6

State Express world team classic

1981	England beat Wales
1982	Canada beat England

Langs Scottish masters

1981	J White beat C Thorburn, 9-4
1982	S Davis beat A Higgins, 9-4

Benson and Hedges masters

1975	J Spencer beat R Reardon, 9-8
1976	R Reardon beat G Miles, 7-3
1977	D Mountjoy beat R Reardon, 7-6
1978	A Higgins beat C Thorburn, 7-5
1979	P Mans beat A Higgins, 8-4
1980	T Griffiths beat A Higgins, 9-5
1981	A Higgins beat T Griffiths, 9-6
1982	S Davis beat T Griffiths, 9-5
1983	C Thorburn beat R Reardon, 9-7

Coral UK championship

1978	D Mountjoy beat David Taylor, 15-9
1979	J Virgo beat T Griffiths, 14-13
1980	S Davis beat A Higgins, 16-6
1981	S Davis beat T Griffiths, 16-3
1982	T Griffiths beat A Higgins, 16-15

Jameson international

1981	S Davis beat Dennis Taylor, 9-0
1982	T Knowles beat David Taylor, 9-6

Pot Black finals

1969	R Reardon beat J Spencer
1970	J Spencer beat R Reardon
1971	E Charlton beat R Reardon
1973	E Charlton beat R Williams
1974	G Miles beat J Spencer
1975	G Miles beat Dennis Taylor
1976	J Spencer beat Dennis Taylor
1977	P Mans beat D Mountjoy
1978	D Mountjoy beat G Miles
1979	R Reardon beat D Mountjoy
1980	E Charlton beat R Reardon
1981	C Thorburn beat J Wych
1982	S Davis beat E Charlton
1983	S Davis beat R Reardon

Acknowledgements

We are most grateful to the World Professional Billiards and Snooker Association and to Sydney Friskin, whose help and advice have been invaluable.

Other suggested reading: *Pot Black* Reg Perrin (BBC Publications), *World Snooker* Jack Karnehm (Pelham), *Guinness Book of Snooker* Clive Everton (Guinness Superlatives).

Additional photographs by: Mary Evans Picture Library (pages 5 and 6); BBC Hulton Picture Library (7, 15, 41); David Muscroft (35, 38, 58, 60, 61); Jim Latham (48, 49, 59)

Alex Higgins